What is Celiac Disease?

Sally & Rob

Best Wishes
Earl Hoffman

✳ Looking forward to
your book :

Table of Contents

What Can You Expect from This Book?

There are currently as many as 3,000,000 Americans living with celiac disease, and as many as 83% of them go undiagnosed. Many people live with the symptoms of celiac disease for months, or years, unaware of the true underlying cause of their health problems. Contrary to popular belief, the main symptoms of celiac disease are not all digestive – there are a number of serious mental and physical symptoms as well. Unfortunately, the symptoms of many autoimmune diseases tend to overlap which makes it difficult to obtain an accurate diagnosis without going through extensive testing.

Many people do not have a complete understanding of what celiac disease is – this is true even for some of the people who have the disease! The purpose of this book is to provide a comprehensive education about celiac disease including its causes, risk factors, symptoms, and treatment options. You'll also learn about the difference between celiac disease and non-celiac gluten sensitivity or intolerance. <u>To give you a more detailed idea of what you'll receive in this book, here is a list of subjects that will be covered:</u>

1. A brief introduction to celiac disease and relevant statistics

2. An overview of autoimmune disease and how celiac fits into the spectrum
3. A detailed description of the mechanism behind the autoimmune celiac response
4. A list of risk factors associated with celiac disease
5. An overview of common signs and symptoms of celiac disease
6. A definition of gluten intolerance and gluten sensitivity
7. An explanation of the difference between gluten intolerance/sensitivity and celiac disease
8. An overview of diagnostic tests and criteria for celiac disease
9. An explanation of treatment options for celiac disease, including the gluten-free diet
10. A list of potential complications related to celiac disease
11. An overview of related conditions for celiac disease and gluten intolerance/sensitivity
12. An introduction to the gluten-free diet and its requirements
13. A detailed list of foods to eat and avoid for celiac disease
14. A brief review of the content covered in this book at the conclusion

Now that you know what you have to look forward to in reading this book, all that is left is to get started! So, don't delay any longer – turn the page and keep reading!

What is Celiac Disease?

    With the gluten-free diet becoming increasingly more popular, awareness about celiac disease is continuing to spread. Even so, however, many people still do not understand exactly what celiac disease is. Many people assume that celiac disease is the same thing as an allergy or that it is similar to a gluten sensitivity or intolerance. In reality, celiac disease is completely different from all of these things, and it may be more prevalent than you realize as well. Current estimates state that as many as 1 in 133 Americans suffer from celiac disease – that is about 1% of the entire U.S. population. But what is celiac disease, really?

    Celiac disease is a type of autoimmune disease that damages the small intestines and inhibits the healthy absorption of nutrients from food. It is also known as sprue, nontropical sprue, gluten intolerance, and gluten-sensitive enteropathy. In order to really understand celiac disease, you need to know the basics about autoimmune disease. Autoimmune diseases like celiac disease affect as many as 50 million Americans, and there are more than 80 different types. An autoimmune disease develops when your own immune system mistakenly identifies healthy cells as foreign invaders and, as a result, launches an attack against them. In essence, your body is attacking itself.

Autoimmune diseases can be very serious and, unfortunately, there is no cure available. Depending on the type of autoimmune disease and the underlying cause, however, there are some treatments which can reduce symptoms. With proper treatment, it is possible for certain autoimmune diseases to go into remission, though the patient may never be fully free from the disease – this is true of celiac disease. It is also worth noting that autoimmune disease can be difficult to diagnose sometimes because the symptoms of many different diseases overlap. Diagnosis of autoimmune disease is usually a multi-stage process at the end of which it may not always be completely clear what the problem is.

Celiac disease is an autoimmune condition that affects the small intestine in particular, and it is triggered by the consumption of gluten. Gluten is a type of protein found in certain grains including wheat, barley, rye, and triticale (a hybrid form of wheat). It can also sometimes be found in other grains that are processed on the same machinery as these grains – this is often the case for oats. In cases of celiac disease, the immune system recognizes gluten as a foreign invader, and they launch an attack against it. Unfortunately, healthy cells and tissues get caught in the crossfire of this attack.

When a person with celiac disease consumes gluten, the body launches an immune response against it, producing toxins designed to destroy the gluten molecules. These toxins also end up damaging the villi that line the small intestine. Villi are very small fingerlike projects that line the walls of the small intestine – they help to absorb nutrients from food as it moves through the digestive system. When those villi are damaged, it becomes more difficult for the body to absorb nutrients from food and that is what causes many of the symptoms associated with celiac disease. Switching to a gluten-free diet usually resolves symptoms for celiac disease patients, though it may take years for their digestive system to fully heal.

What are the Risk Factors for Celiac Disease?

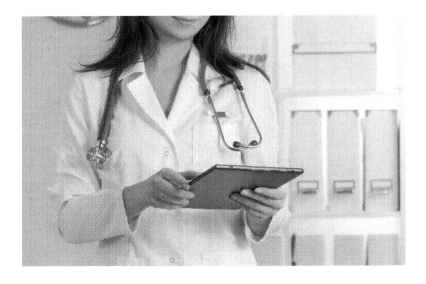

Though anyone could technically develop celiac disease, it tends to run in families – this is true for many autoimmune conditions. In fact, the University of Chicago Medical Center states that people who have a parent or sibling with celiac disease have a 1 in 22 chance of developing the condition themselves. You are also more likely to develop celiac disease if you have another autoimmune condition or certain kinds of genetic disorders.

Some of the autoimmune and genetic diseases which may increase your risk for celiac disease include the following:

- Addison's disease
- Down syndrome
- Intestinal cancer
- Lactose intolerance
- Lupus
- Rheumatoid arthritis
- Sjogren's syndrome
- Thyroid disease
- Turner syndrome
- Type 1 diabetes

There is also some evidence to suggest that environmental factors including early feeding practices could impact a child's risk of developing celiac disease. In an article published in the *Italian Journal of Pediatrics* in August 2015, "Infant feeding and weaning practices, as well as timing of gluten introduction in the diet, have been suggested to contribute" to celiac disease risk. In 2006, an analysis of six case studies was made to determine whether there was a link between the duration of breastfeeding and a reduced risk for celiac disease. According to the results of this study, breastfeeding seemed to offer protective benefits in terms of developing celiac disease. The results were not conclusive, but they did suggest a connection.

Another study seemed to indicate that, for infants and first-degree relatives of patients diagnosed with celiac disease, introducing gluten for the first time between the ages of 4 and 6 months was correlated with a lower risk for celiac disease than introductions made earlier or later than this age. Furthermore, exposure to small qualities of gluten at 16 to 24 weeks of age (while breastfeeding) was shown to reduce the frequency of celiac disease at age three. Again, more research is required (and is being conducted) to see whether these results are truly significant and whether they might point toward preventive measures for this autoimmune disease.

What are the Signs and Symptoms of Celiac Disease?

Celiac disease is a condition that primarily affects the small intestine. Many of the symptoms related to celiac disease are digestive in nature, but not all of them. In many cases, the symptoms start out as digestive problems but the longer the condition goes undiagnosed, the more the symptoms spread throughout the body. It is also worth mentioning that celiac disease symptoms sometimes look different in children than in adults.

To give you an idea what symptoms for celiac disease look like, here is a list of the symptoms that most commonly appear in the early stages of celiac disease:

- Abdominal bloating
- Gas
- Chronic diarrhea
- Constipation

- Pale stools
- Foul-smelling stools
- Stomach pain
- Nausea and vomiting

The longer you continue to consume gluten, the more compounded your symptoms will become. A failure to absorb nutrients from the food you eat over a period of weeks, months, or years can be very significant. <u>Here are some of the other symptoms commonly associated with long-term celiac disease</u>:

- Failure to thrive (infants)
- Delayed puberty (adolescents)
- Stunted growth
- Irritability
- Weight loss
- Chronic fatigue
- Anemia
- Depression or anxiety
- Osteoporosis
- Joint pain
- Chronic headaches
- Sores inside the mouth
- Infertility
- Frequent miscarriages
- Missed menstrual periods
- Tingling hands and feet

As you can see, some of the symptoms of celiac disease are fairly broad and may overlap with the symptoms of other diseases. Another symptom that may occur with celiac disease is called dermatitis herpetiformis (DH) – it is a type of very itchy skin rash that produces both bumps and blisters. This rash usually forms on the elbows, knees, and buttocks and it occurs in about 15 to 25 percent of people with celiac disease. People who develop DH typically don't exhibit digestive symptoms related to their celiac disease. In fact, some people with celiac disease don't exhibit any symptoms at all. They can still be affected by long-term complications related to the malabsorption of nutrients, however.

Celiac Disease Symptoms Questionnaire

The only way to receive an official diagnosis of celiac disease is to speak to your doctor and to undergo a series of tests –

you'll learn about the diagnostic criteria for celiac disease in a later chapter. For now, however, you might be curious to see how your symptoms line up with the common symptoms of celiac disease. Take this celiac disease symptoms questionnaire to find out. Once you complete the questionnaire, you can take it with you to your doctor visit so you can accurately describe the symptoms you've been experiencing.

1. Do you have a first-degree relative (parent, sibling, child) with celiac disease?

    Yes   No   Unsure

2. Do you have a second-degree relative (aunt, uncle, grandparent, niece, nephew, cousin, or half-sibling) with celiac disease?

    Yes   No   Unsure

3. Do you suffer from frequent abdominal gas, bloating, or stomach pain?

    Yes   No   Unsure

4. Do you have pale, or foul-smelling stools?

    Yes   No   Unsure

5. Do you experience frequent nausea or vomiting?

    Yes   No   Unsure

6. Do you notice any of these symptoms worsening with gluten consumption?

    Yes   No   Unsure

7. Do you feel tired all the time, despite getting plenty of sleep?

    Yes   No   Unsure

8. Do you suffer from joint pain or have you been diagnosed with osteoporosis?

     Yes   No   Unsure

9. Do you suffer from frequent headaches or migraines?

     Yes   No   Unsure

10. Do you have trouble with new or worsening depression or anxiety?

     Yes   No   Unsure

11. Have you had a miscarriage, fertility problems, or missed menstrual periods?

     Yes   No   Unsure

12. Do you often notice a tingling feeling in your hands and feet?

     Yes   No   Unsure

13. Do you often feel as though your brain is "foggy"?

     Yes   No   Unsure

14. Do you find yourself becoming more irritable or angry than usual?

     Yes   No   Unsure

15. Have you lost weight without really trying?

     Yes   No   Unsure

16. Do you have trouble digesting dairy products like milk or ice cream?

     Yes   No   Unsure

17. Have you noticed an itchy skin rash on your knees, elbows, or buttocks?

Yes   No   Unsure

18. Do you have any other autoimmune disorders or diseases? Circle all that apply.

Addison's disease

Autoimmune hepatitis

Crohn's disease

Chronic pancreatitis

Down syndrome

Idiopathic dilated cardiomyopathy

IgA nephropathy

Inflammatory bowel disease

Irritable bowel syndrome

Juvenile idiopathic arthritis

Multiple sclerosis

Primary biliary cirrhosis

Primary sclerosing cholangitis

Psoriasis

Rheumatoid arthritis

Scleroderma

Sjogren's syndrome

Thyroid disease

Turner syndrome

Type 1 diabetes

Ulcerative colitis

Williams syndrome

How is Celiac Disease Different from a Gluten Intolerance or a Gluten Sensitivity?

It is fairly common for people who don't have celiac disease to misunderstand it – they often assume that it is simply another level of gluten sensitivity or intolerance. There is a big difference, however, in the way gluten ingestion affects the body with celiac disease versus gluten intolerance or sensitivity. There is also a major difference between celiac disease and a wheat allergy. A wheat allergy is an immune response triggered by any of the proteins found in wheat (gluten is one), but it affects the body differently than celiac disease.

Wheat allergy symptoms usually occur within minutes of consuming wheat, though they could be delayed by up to two hours. The symptoms of wheat allergy usually include diarrhea, nausea, vomiting, hives or rash, nasal congestion, eye irritation, and difficulty breathing. As is true with any allergy, the severity can range from mild to life-threatening. In severe cases, a wheat allergy could trigger anaphylaxis or severe breathing difficulty. If a wheat allergy is that severe, the patient will typically carry an epinephrine auto-injector or EpiPen. Using the EpiPen after accidentally ingesting wheat will prevent anaphylaxis.

Now, regarding the differences between celiac disease and gluten sensitivity or intolerance. There is a great deal of controversy out there regarding the existence of gluten sensitivities, primarily because scientists still don't fully understand the cause of the biological reaction. Also known as non-celiac gluten sensitivity (NCGS), there is no test for a gluten sensitivity or intolerance. People who have this condition might experience negative symptoms after eating gluten, but they don't test positive for celiac disease or a wheat allergy. The most common symptoms reported for NCGS include brain fog, chronic fatigue, gas, bloating, abdominal pain, and headaches.

Although there is no test that can diagnose a non-celiac gluten sensitivity, your doctor can order tests to rule out celiac disease or a wheat allergy. If both of those tests are negative, your doctor might recommend a trial period in which you avoid eating gluten-containing foods. If that solves the problem, the chances are good that you have some kind of sensitivity or intolerance to gluten that doesn't go as far as celiac disease or a full-blown allergy. You might also want to keep an eye out for other symptoms and, if necessary, be tested for other autoimmune diseases because there is a correlation with gluten sensitivity.

How is Celiac Disease Diagnosed?

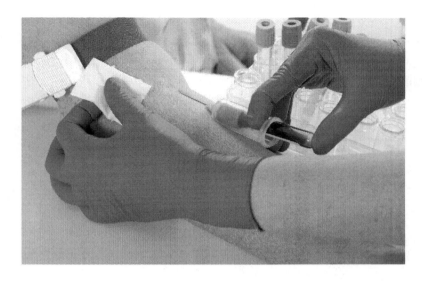

There is no one test that can diagnose celiac disease. In order to obtain a complete diagnosis, you'll have to have your doctor perform a physical exam and then you'll have to have blood drawn to run a series of tests. Depending on the results of those tests, your doctor may also request an endoscopy or intestinal biopsy to confirm celiac disease. As you may remember from an earlier section, diagnosing celiac disease can be tricky because some people don't display symptoms and others display symptoms that overlap with a variety of other conditions. In fact, the University of Chicago Medicine Celiac Disease Center reports that the average length of time it takes to diagnose celiac disease is four years. Unfortunately, this delay can also increase your risk of developing other health problems including neurological disorders, osteoporosis, other autoimmune diseases, and cancer.

When you go to see your doctor about potentially diagnosing celiac disease, you'll want to have a list of symptoms to bring with you. Your doctor will want to know which symptoms you've been experiencing when they began, and whether they seem to get better or worse when you eat certain foods. Given this information, your doctor will perform a physical exam to judge the severity of physical symptoms and to help rule out other medical causes for your symptoms. If your symptoms still seem to be consistent with celiac and your doctor can't find any other problems, you'll likely move on to blood tests. The most common blood tests used to indicate celiac disease include the following:

- **Tissue Transglutaminase Antibodies Test** – Also known as a tTG-IgA test, this blood test looks for the type of antibody produced by the immune system to fight against gluten. It will only be present if you are still eating gluten, so you shouldn't switch to a gluten-free diet until all of your tests have been completed. This test will be positive in 98% of patients with celiac disease, and it will be negative in 95% of people who don't have celiac disease.
- **IgA Endomysial Antibody Test** – Also known as an IgA EMA test, this test is a little less sensitive than the previous test, and it is typically used to diagnose difficult patients because it is expensive and requires the use of human umbilical cord or primate esophagus. This test is positive in 90% to 95% of celiac patients.
- **Total Serum IgA Test** – This test is used to diagnose an IgA deficiency – this is a condition frequently associated with celiac disease patients, and it has the potential to cause a false negative result for tTg-IgA or EMA tests.
- **Deaminated Gliadin Peptide Test** – This test is usually reserved for individuals who test positive for IgA deficiency or who test negative for tTg and EMA antibodies.

If you are one of the 25% of celiac patients who develop DH, your doctor may request a skin biopsy. During the biopsy, the doctor will carefully remove small samples of skin tissue and examine them under a microscope. If the results of the biopsy and the results of your blood tests all seem to indicate celiac disease, the testing might end there. If your blood test results are inconclusive and you don't have a DH rash, it may be necessary to take things to the next level – an endoscopy.

An endoscopy is a minor surgical procedure that doesn't involve an incision. Your doctor will take a small, thin tube called an endoscope and thread it through your mouth, down your esophagus, and into your intestines – you will be put under general anesthesia for the procedure. At the end of the tube, there is a small camera that your doctor will use to check the lining of your intestines for damage to the villi. If there appears to be damage, your doctor may also take a small sample of intestinal tissue for a biopsy analysis to confirm the diagnosis of celiac disease. If there is no damage and your blood tests were inconclusive, it would seem unlikely that you have celiac disease. You may still have some form of sensitivity or intolerance, but it is unlikely to have any autoimmune component.

What Treatments are Available for Celiac Disease?

Once your doctor has confirmed a diagnosis of celiac disease, you must start following a gluten-free diet. There is no medication for celiac disease and no supplements you can take to stave off intestinal damage. Autoimmune diseases like celiac disease have no cure, but it is possible to go into remission with proper treatment. The only treatment for celiac disease that is guaranteed to work is committing to a gluten-free diet. This involves removing foods from your diet that contain gluten – all forms of wheat, barley, and rye.

To help you make the switch and then stick to a completely gluten-free diet, here are some steps you should take:

- Learn about the foods in which gluten can be found – refer to the food lists provided in this book.
- Learn how to read a food label so you can tell whether a product contains gluten or not – not all foods are going to say

"gluten-free" and gluten may not be listed in the allergen warning.

- Remove all sources of gluten-containing foods from your home or, if you live with other non-celiac individuals, clear out a cupboard to store your own food.
- Purchase new food preparation supplies that are difficult to clean (like cutting boards, plastic or wooden utensils, colanders, etc.) and keep your own for gluten-free food prep.
- Buy separate dishwashing supplies to clean plates, utensils, and other containers used for your gluten-free food.
- If you live with other people and share a refrigerator or other kitchen space, label all of your personal foods "gluten-free" and make sure that no one else uses them.
- When using foods from a multi-serving container (like a jar of peanut butter), always use a clean utensil to avoid cross-contact.

Following a gluten-free diet can be tricky at first while you're still learning about the foods that contain gluten. Add to that the challenge of avoiding cross-contact with foods and surfaces that have been exposed to gluten, and you may become frustrated. Just keep reminding yourself that sticking to a gluten-free diet is the only way you're going to experience relief from your symptoms. When you've been following a gluten-free diet for a few weeks you may be surprised at how much better you feel – you may have been experiencing symptoms related to your celiac disease that you didn't even know were happening.

The longer you stick to your gluten-free diet, the better you are going to feel. Unfortunately, this might also mean that if you slip up somewhere down the road and accidentally eat something with gluten in it, your reaction could be very severe. People who have been closely following a gluten-free diet for years at a time often find this to be true. That is why it is so important that once you start following a gluten-free diet that you really commit to it. If you are exposed to gluten (this is often referred to as "being glutened"), you are probably going to feel it pretty quickly. Unfortunately, there is nothing you can do to immediately counteract the effects of the gluten consumption.

If you accidentally ingest gluten, even a little bit, there are certain things you can do to recover more quickly. Nothing will have an immediate impact on relieving symptoms of gluten consumption, but taking care of yourself properly will help to minimize your distress and may help you to get back to feeling normal more quickly. <u>Here are some simple things you can do to speed your recovery after accidentally ingesting gluten</u>:

- **Take it easy**. You are going to feel pretty miserable for a while, so give yourself time to rest by taking time off work or by relying on friends and family to lend a helping hand.
- **Make yourself comfortable**. Put on some loose-fitting clothing in case you experience bloating, run a hot shower, or warm up a heating pad to deal with stomach cramps. You might also find it soothing to soak in an Epsom salt bath.
- **Get some sleep**. In order to recover from being glutened you're going to need to sleep. You'll probably feel pretty fatigued anyway, so give yourself some extra time for sleep!
- **Drink plenty of fluids**. Drinking a lot of water and other liquids will help to settle your stomach and help to flush toxins out of your system. If you don't like plain water, try lemon water, coconut water, herbal tea, or pomegranate juice.
- **Avoid heavy meals**. While your body is recovering from accidental ingestion, you're going to want to eat light meals, so you don't compound the digestive issues. Stick to naturally gluten-free foods as well, avoiding processed and prepared foods.
- **Take some supplements if they help**. If you need a little something to help you get through your day, that is perfectly fine. Some people find that ibuprofen helps to reduce inflammation and digestive enzymes or probiotics help them to feel better sooner.

- **Give yourself some grace**. Don't beat yourself up over your mistake, especially if it wasn't your fault. And remember that depression and anxiety can sometimes be symptoms of celiac disease, so be on the lookout for changes in mood after you accidentally ingest gluten.
- **Be open with your loved ones**. If you know that you're going to be miserable for the next few days, speak up and tell your friends and family! If there is some way that they can help, don't be afraid to ask and don't isolate yourself if you know that it will only make things worse.

Every person is different, so your body might not respond to accidental gluten ingestion in the same way that someone else's does. Unfortunately, it is just something you'll have to learn when it happens. The first time you accidentally eat gluten, make a note of your symptoms and how quickly they progress so you know what to look for the next time. You should also try out some of these tips to see what works for you and what doesn't so you know what to focus on the next time it happens.

Related Conditions and Complications

By now you know fully well what celiac disease and what it looks like. You also know that it is easy to confuse celiac disease with other diseases, particularly other autoimmune conditions. In this section, we're going to review some of the conditions that are often confused for celiac disease as well as some of the complications that could result from long-term untreated celiac disease. <u>Here is an overview of some of the other diseases and conditions commonly confused with celiac disease</u>:

- **Acid Reflux** – When the contents of your stomach back up into your esophagus, it is called acid reflux. Chronic reflux can lead to digestive symptoms like abdominal bloating and may also cause headaches which can sometimes be confused for celiac disease or other food sensitivities.
- **Addison's Disease** – This is a condition characterized by the insufficient production of hormones by the adrenal glands. Symptoms of Addison's disease include chronic fatigue,

weight loss, nausea, diarrhea, vomiting, abdominal pain, joint pain, and irritability or depression.

- **Crohn's Disease** – A chronic digestive disorder, Crohn's disease is characterized by inflammation, swelling, and sores in the lining of the digestive tract. This condition tends to run in families and may produce symptoms like diarrhea, abdominal pain, and unexplained weight loss.
- **Down Syndrome** – This is a genetic condition caused by abnormal cell division which results in either an extra or an irregular chromosome. Children with down syndrome often grow more slowly than healthy children, a symptom which overlaps with childhood celiac disease.
- **Irritable Bowel Syndrome** – Also known as IBS, irritable bowel syndrome causes belly pain, cramping, bloating, and diarrhea or constipation. This is a long-term condition in which symptoms may vary from day to day, but it generally doesn't worsen over time.
- **Iron Deficiency Anemia** – This condition develops when there isn't enough iron in your blood, and it can make you feel weak, tired, and irritable. These symptoms often overlap with the symptoms of celiac disease.
- **Osteoporosis** – This is a condition in which the bones become thin, brittle, and easy to break. These symptoms are easily confused with the results of malnutrition caused by celiac-related malabsorption of nutrients.
- **Rheumatoid Arthritis** – A chronic inflammatory disorder, rheumatoid arthritis occurs when the immune system starts to attack the joints. In addition to causing joint pain, RA can also present with symptoms including chronic fatigue, weight loss, and fever.
- **Type 1 Diabetes** – An autoimmune condition that causes the pancreas to stop producing insulin, type 1 diabetes can lead to problems with the heart, eyes, nerves, and kidneys. Symptoms are typically correlated with meals, depending on the glycemic load.

- **Thyroid Disease** – Hashimoto's disease is the most common type of hypothyroidism or underactive thyroid gland. Symptoms of Hashimoto's disease include fatigue, joint pain, constipation, depression, and weight gain.
- **Sjogren's Syndrome** – This is a condition in which the immune system targets the tear and saliva glands, causing them to become scarred and damaged. This condition can sometimes cause chronic fatigue and joint pain.

Not only can other autoimmune conditions be confused with celiac disease, but the long-term untreated celiac disease can actually increase your risk of developing any of these conditions. There are also some complications which have been associated with celiac disease as both an autoimmune and digestive disorder. The most common complication of celiac disease is malnutrition that results from an inability to absorb nutrients from food – this happens when the villi lining your small intestine become damaged by autoimmune activity.

Malnutrition can contribute to bone loss, and the damage to the villi might also contribute to lactose intolerance. Children with celiac disease have a high risk for developing irritability, depression, or other mood disorders and adults frequently develop problems with memory and concentration as well as chronic fatigue. If left untreated for long enough, celiac disease can contribute to the development of lymphoma or bowel cancer and, in pregnant women, it can lead to low birth weight for babies. Fortunately, many of the symptoms of celiac disease start to improve within a few weeks on a gluten-free diet.

Understanding the Gluten-Free Diet

If you have been diagnosed with celiac disease, gluten intolerance, or gluten sensitivity, the best treatment is to avoid consuming gluten. While many people treat the gluten-free diet like another fad diet, for the aforementioned individuals it is actually a medical necessity. Avoiding gluten is the only way to prevent your body from launching an autoimmune response, and it is the only way to give your body time to heal from the intestinal damage caused by such a response.

While there are some foods in which gluten is "hidden," many gluten-free foods are completely natural and easy to identify. For example, all fruits and vegetables are naturally gluten-free, as are nuts, seeds, meat, poultry, and fish. You'll have to be careful when it comes to grains since there are many forms of wheat which go by other names – there are also some grains which could be cross-contaminated with gluten because they have been processed on shared equipment. It is best to be safe rather than sorry.

You also can't count on food manufacturers to label their products as gluten-free or to identify gluten as a potential allergen. Manufacturers are required to list wheat as an allergen if wheat products are used in the food, but not all sources of gluten come from wheat. Even more confusing is the fact that the opposite may also be true – ingredients like wheat starch may come from wheat but are often processed to remove gluten to below 20 ppm. You'll need to educate yourself about the different forms of wheat, barley, and rye and take a look at the different types of food in which gluten may be hidden. In the next section, you'll find a collection of detailed lists of foods you should avoid and safe foods to eat.

List of Foods to Eat and Avoid

When you are first diagnosed with celiac disease, switching to a gluten-free diet can be a challenge. If you follow the typical Western diet which is heavy in processed foods and refined carbohydrates, gluten is probably a staple of your diet. The good news is that while learning about the different forms of wheat, barley, and rye, as well as other hidden sources of gluten, might take some time, once you know what to look for, it's actually pretty easy to pick out gluten-free foods.

To help you get started, here are some lists of foods you should avoid on the gluten-free diet as well as some safe foods:

Avoid: Grains Containing Gluten

- Wheat
- Wheatberries
- Durum
- Emmer

- Semolina
- Spelt
- Farina
- Farro
- Graham
- Kamut
- Einkorn wheat
- Rye
- Barley
- Triticale
- Malt
- Malted barley flour
- Malted milk
- Malt extract
- Malt syrup
- Malt flavoring
- Malt vinegar
- Brewer's Yeast
- Wheat starch (sometimes)

Avoid: Foods Made with Gluten-Containing Grains*

*These are foods which are commonly made with gluten-containing grains but some versions of these foods may be made gluten-free

- All-purpose flour
- Baked goods
- Baking mix
- Bread
- Bagels
- Beer
- Biscuits
- Brewer's yeast
- Breading
- Breadcrumbs
- Brownies
- Brown rice syrup
- Cakes
- Cake flour
- Cake mix
- Candy/candy bars
- Cheesecake filling
- Croissants
- Cornbread
- Cookies
- Crepes
- Cereal
- Cereal bars
- Croutons
- Couscous
- Donuts
- Graham crackers
- Granola
- Gravy
- Gnocchi
- Energy bars
- Flatbreads
- French toast
- French fries
- Potato chips
- Tortilla chips

- Multigrain chips
- Imitation crab meat
- Lunchmeat
- Muffin mix
- Pancakes
- Pancake mix
- Pretzels
- Protein bars
- Pita bread
- Pastry flour
- Pasta
- Egg noodles
- Ramen noodles
- Udon noodles
- Soba noodles
- Soup
- Salad dressing
- Self-basting poultry
- Marinades
- Meat substitutes
- Naan bread
- Potato bread
- Rolls
- Stuffing
- Sauces
- Soy sauce
- Tortillas (flour)
- Waffles
- Whole-wheat flour

Eat: Fresh Fruits and Vegetables

- Acorn Squash
- Apples
- Apricots
- Asparagus
- Artichoke
- Arugula
- Banana
- Beets
- Bell Peppers
- Bok Choy
- Blackberries
- Blueberries
- Broccoli
- Brussels Sprouts
- Butternut Squash
- Cabbage
- Carrots
- Cantaloupe
- Cauliflower
- Celery
- Cherries
- Cranberries
- Cucumber
- Dates
- Eggplant
- Fennel
- Figs
- Grapes

- Grapefruit
- Greens
- Green Beans
- Green Onion
- Guava
- Honeydew
- Kale
- Kohlrabi
- Kiwi
- Lemon
- Lettuce
- Lime
- Leeks
- Mango
- Mushrooms
- Nectarines
- Onions
- Papaya
- Parsnips
- Peaches
- Pears
- Pineapple
- Plums
- Pomegranate
- Pumpkin
- Raspberries
- Rutabaga
- Snow Peas
- Spaghetti Squash
- Spinach
- Strawberries
- Snap Peas
- Sweet Potato
- Tomatoes
- Turnips
- Watercress
- Watermelon
- Zucchini

Eat: Beans, Legumes, and Gluten-Free Grains

- Amaranth
- Arborio rice
- Black beans
- Brown rice
- Buckwheat
- Cannellini beans
- Chickpeas
- Corn
- Cornmeal
- Kidney beans
- Lentils
- Millet
- Oats
- Pinto beans
- Quinoa
- Split peas
- Sorghum
- Soybeans
- Teff
- White beans
- White rice
- Wild rice

Eat: Nuts, Seeds, and Oils

- Almonds
- Almond Butter
- Avocado
- Avocado Oil
- Brazil Nuts
- Cashews
- Chestnuts
- Chia Seeds
- Clarified Butter
- Coconut Milk
- Coconut Oil
- Flaxseeds
- Flaxseed Oil
- Hazelnuts
- Hemp Seeds
- Lard
- Macadamia Nuts
- Olives
- Olive Oil
- Pecans
- Pine Nuts
- Pistachios
- Pumpkin Seeds
- Sesame Oil
- Sesame Seeds
- Sunflower Seeds
- Tallow
- Walnuts
- Walnut Oil

Eat: Eggs, Meat, Poultry, Fish and Seafood

- Anchovy
- Bacon
- Bass
- Beef
- Bison
- Catfish
- Chicken
- Crab
- Clams
- Cod
- Duck
- Eel
- Eggs
- Fish
- Flounder
- Goat
- Haddock
- Halibut
- Hake
- Herring
- Lamb
- Lobster
- Mackerel
- Mahi-Mahi
- Mussels
- Oysters
- Perch
- Pollock
- Salmon
- Sardines
- Sausage
- Scad
- Scallops
- Shark

- Shrimp
- Seabass
- Sole
- Snapper
- Swordfish
- Tilapia
- Trout
- Tuna
- Veal
- Venison

Eat: Dairy Products

- Butter
- Buttermilk
- Cheese (except blue cheese)
- Coffee creamer
- Cottage cheese
- Condensed milk
- Cream
- Cream cheese
- Crème Fraiche
- Custard
- Dried milk
- Dulce de Leche
- Evaporated milk
- Frozen custard
- Frozen yogurt
- Gelato
- Goat's milk
- Half n' Half
- Heavy cream
- Ice cream
- Kefir
- Milk
- Quark
- Whey
- Whipped cream
- Yogurt

Eat: Baking Staples and Alternative Flours

- Almond flour
- Almond meal
- Almond milk
- Apple cider vinegar
- Arrowroot powder
- Baking powder
- Baking soda
- Balsamic vinegar

- Broth
- Brown rice flour
- Cocoa powder
- Coconut aminos
- Coconut flour
- Coconut milk
- Coconut palm sugar
- Cornmeal
- Cornstarch
- Dark chocolate
- Fresh herbs
- Ground spices
- Honey
- Maple syrup
- Potato flour
- Potato starch
- Rice flour
- Stevia
- Tapioca flour
- Tapioca starch
- Vanilla extract

Sample Gluten-Free Recipes

<u>Recipes Included in this Section</u>:

Mediterranean Style Frittata

Coconut Flour Banana
Pancakes

Tomato Basil Omelet

Almond Flour Blueberry
Muffins

Spinach Salad with Bacon
Dressing

Creamy Butternut Squash
Soup

Chicken Salad with Grapes
and Pecans

Hearty Beef and Bean Chili

Almond-Crusted Halibut

Rosemary Roasted Chicken
and Veggies

Cilantro Turkey Burgers

Balsamic Glazed Salmon

Cheesy Chicken Casserole

BBQ-Glazed Meatloaf

Avocado Chocolate Mousse

Ginger Peach Crisp

Coconut Flour Fudge
Brownies

Almond Coconut Cupcakes

Mediterranean Style Frittata

Servings: 4 to 6

Ingredients:

- 10 large eggs
- ½ cup skim milk
- Salt and pepper to taste
- 2 tablespoons olive oil, divided
- 1 medium zucchini, diced
- 1 small red onion, diced
- 2 cups cherry or grape tomatoes, whole
- 1 teaspoon dried oregano
- ½ cup crumbled feta cheese
- ¼ cup sliced black olives

Instructions:

1. Preheat the oven to 400°F.
2. In a medium bowl, whisk together the eggs, milk, salt, and pepper.
3. Pour half the olive oil into a cast iron skillet and heat it over medium-high heat.
4. Add the zucchini and onion and sauté for 5 minutes until lightly browned.
5. Remove the veggies to a bowl and reheat the skillet with the rest of the oil.
6. Add the tomatoes and cook until they start to burst.
7. Spoon the zucchini and onion back into the skillet and season with salt and pepper.
8. Pour in the egg mixture then sprinkle with oregano, feta cheese, and olives.
9. Cook for 3 minutes then transfer to the oven and cook for 15 to 20 minutes until the eggs are just set.
10. Broil the frittata for a few minutes to brown the top then cool 5 minutes before slicing to serve.

Coconut Flour Banana Pancakes

Servings: 4

Ingredients:

- 2 cups skim milk
- 8 large eggs, beaten well
- 1 tablespoon vanilla extract
- Stevia extract to taste
- 2 large bananas, peeled and mashed
- 1 cup coconut flour
- 2 teaspoons baking soda
- 1 teaspoon salt

Instructions:

1. In a medium mixing bowl, whisk together your milk, eggs, vanilla extract and stevia.
2. Stir in the mashed banana along with the coconut flour, baking soda, and salt.
3. Keep stirring until the mixture is smooth then let it rest for 10 minutes.
4. Grease a large skillet with cooking spray then spoon the batter into the pan, using about 3 tablespoons per pancake.
5. Let the pancakes cook until bubbles form in the surface of the batter.
6. Flip the pancakes and cook until they are just browned on the other side.
7. Transfer the pancakes to a plate to keep warm and repeat with the remaining batter.
8. Serve the pancakes warm with maple syrup or honey.

Tomato Basil Omelet

Servings: 1

Ingredients:

- 3 large eggs
- 1 tablespoon milk
- 1 tablespoon fresh chopped chives
- Salt and pepper to taste
- 1 medium tomato, cored and chopped
- ¼ cup diced yellow onion
- 1 clove minced garlic
- 1 tablespoon fresh chopped basil

Instructions:

1. In a medium bowl, whisk together the eggs, milk, chives, salt and pepper.
2. Pour half the olive oil into a medium skillet and heat it over medium heat.
3. Add the onions, tomatoes, and garlic then sauté for 5 minutes until tender.
4. Spread the mixture evenly in the skillet then pour in the egg mixture.
5. Cook for 2 minutes then sprinkle on the basil and cook for 1 minute more.
6. When the egg is halfway set, fold half the omelet over itself.
7. Cook the egg until it is done to the desired level then slide onto a plate to serve.

Almond Flour Blueberry Muffins

Servings: 12

Ingredients:

- 4 cups almond flour
- 1 teaspoon baking soda
- 1 teaspoon salt
- 4 large eggs, whisked

- ½ cup agave syrup
- 3 tablespoons apple cider vinegar
- ¼ cup olive oil
- 1 tablespoon vanilla extract
- 1 ½ cups fresh blueberries

Instructions:

1. Preheat the oven to 350°F and line a muffin pan with paper liners.
2. Combine the almond flour, baking soda and salt in a mixing bowl and stir well.
3. In a separate bowl, whisk together the eggs, agave syrup, cider vinegar, olive oil, and vanilla extract.
4. Stir the wet ingredients into the dry until just combined then fold in the blueberries.
5. Spoon the batter into the pan evenly and bake for 20 to 25 minutes until a knife inserted in a muffin comes out clean.
6. Cool the muffins for 5 minutes in the pan then cool the rest of the way on a wire rack.

Spinach and Mushroom Omelet

Servings: 1

Ingredients:

- 3 large eggs
- 1 tablespoon milk
- 1 green onion, sliced thin
- Salt and pepper to taste
- ½ cup diced mushrooms
- ¼ small onion, chopped
- 1 clove minced garlic
- 1 cup chopped spinach

Instructions:

1. In a medium bowl, whisk together the eggs, milk, green onion, salt, and pepper.
2. Pour half the olive oil into a medium skillet and heat it over medium heat.
3. Add the mushrooms, onions, and garlic then sauté for 5 minutes until tender.
4. Stir in the spinach and cook until it is just wilted.
5. Spread the mixture evenly in the skillet then pour in the egg mixture.
6. Cook for 3 minutes then fold half the omelet over itself.
7. Let the egg cook until it is done to the desired level then slide onto a plate to serve.

Spinach Salad with Bacon Dressing
Servings: 4

Ingredients:

- 2 large eggs
- 6 slices bacon, uncooked
- 1 small red onion, sliced thin
- 8 ounces sliced mushrooms
- 6 cups fresh baby spinach
- 2 tablespoons red wine vinegar
- 1 ½ teaspoons sugar
- 1 teaspoon Dijon mustard

Instructions:

1. Place the eggs in a saucepan and cover with water.
2. Bring the water to a boil then remove from heat and let sit for 20 minutes.
3. Transfer the eggs to an ice bath to cool then peel and slice them.
4. Cook the bacon in a skillet over medium-high heat until crispy.

5. Remove the bacon to a paper towel to drain then spoon off 4 tablespoons of the bacon grease.
6. Add 2 tablespoons of the grease to a separate skillet and heat it over medium heat.
7. Sauté the onions in the bacon grease until browned then add the mushrooms and cook until they are browned as well.
8. Once the bacon is cool, chop it and set it aside.
9. Add the remaining 2 tablespoons of bacon grease to a small bowl and whisk in the vinegar, sugar, and Dijon mustard until smooth.
10. Divide the spinach among 4 salad plates and top with sliced eggs, mushrooms, and onions.
11. Drizzle each salad with dressing and top with chopped bacon to serve.

Creamy Butternut Squash Soup

Servings: 6 to 8

Ingredients:

- 2 large butternut squash
- 2 tablespoons olive oil
- Salt and pepper
- 1 tablespoon coconut oil
- 2 medium onions, sliced thin
- 1-inch fresh grated ginger
- 3 cloves minced garlic
- 6 cups chicken broth
- ½ cup heavy cream

Instructions:

1. Preheat the oven to 375°F and line a rimmed baking sheet with foil.
2. Cut the squash in half then scoop out and discard the seeds.

3. Peel the squash then cut the flesh into chunks and place it in a large bowl.
4. Toss the squash with the olive oil then spread on the baking sheet – season with salt and pepper.
5. Roast for 30 to 45 minutes until tender then remove from the oven.
6. Heat the coconut oil in a large stockpot over medium heat.
7. Add the onion, ginger, and garlic and cook for 12 minutes until the onion is browned and softened.
8. Add the squash along with the chicken broth and bring to a boil.
9. Reduce heat and simmer for 15 minutes, covered.
10. Remove from heat and puree the soup using an immersion blender until smooth.
11. Stir in the cream and season with salt and pepper to taste.

Chicken Salad with Grapes and Pecans

Servings: 4 to 6

Ingredients:

- 2 pounds boneless skinless chicken tenderloins
- ½ cup olive oil mayonnaise
- ½ cup light sour cream
- 1 tablespoon lemon juice
- 1 tablespoon Dijon mustard
- Salt and pepper to taste
- 2 cups red seedless grapes, halved
- 1 cup chopped pecans
- ½ cup diced celery
- ¼ cup sliced green onion

Instructions:

1. Bring a pot of lightly salted water to boil.

2. Add the chicken tenderloins and cook until they are no longer pink.
3. Drain the chicken and let it cool, then chop or shred it.
4. In a medium bowl, whisk together the mayonnaise with the sour cream, lemon juice, Dijon mustard, salt, and pepper.
5. Add the chicken along with the grapes, pecans, celery and green onion.
6. Toss it all together until evenly coated then chill until ready to serve.
7. Serve on toasted gluten-free bread or over a bed of chopped lettuce.

Hearty Beef and Bean Chili

Servings: 6

Ingredients:

1 tablespoon coconut oil

- 2 large yellow onion, chopped
- 2 jalapeno, seeded and sliced thin
- 6 cloves minced garlic
- 2 pounds lean ground beef
- ¼ cup chili powder
- 2 tablespoons brown sugar
- 1 ½ tablespoons ground cumin
- 2 teaspoons paprika
- 2 (14-ounce) cans diced tomatoes
- 2 (15-ounce) cans beans (your choice)
- 2 cups beef broth

Instructions:

1. Heat the oil in a large pot over medium-high heat.
2. Add the onions and cook for 5 minutes until browned then stir in the jalapeno and garlic – sauté for 1 minutes.

3. Stir in the ground beef and cook until browned, breaking it into chunks with a wooden spoon.
4. Drain the fat then stir in the brown sugar and spices along with the tomatoes, beans, and broth.
5. Bring the mixture to a boil then reduce heat and simmer for 45 minutes.
6. Skim any extra fat from the top of the chili then serve hot topped with diced red onion and shredded cheddar cheese.

Almond-Crusted Halibut

Servings: 4

Ingredients:

- 4 (6-ounce) boneless halibut fillets
- Salt and pepper
- ½ cup almond flour
- ¼ cup finely chopped almonds
- 1 tablespoon dried parsley
- Fresh lemon wedges

Instructions:

1. Preheat the oven to 425°F and line a baking sheet with foil.
2. Season the halibut fillets with salt and pepper.
3. Combine the almond flour, chopped almonds, and parsley in a shallow dish.
4. Dredge the fish fillets in the almond mixture, coating both sides, then place them on the baking sheet.
5. Bake the fish for 12 to 16 minutes until cooked to the desired level.
6. Serve the halibut fillets hot with lemon wedges.

Rosemary Roasted Chicken and Veggies

Servings: 6

Ingredients:

- 2 medium sweet potatoes, chopped
- 1 cup broccoli florets
- 1 medium zucchini, sliced
- 1 cup baby carrots
- 1 large yellow onion, sliced thick
- ½ cup chicken broth
- 1 tablespoon dried rosemary
- 1 teaspoon dried thyme
- Salt and pepper
- 1 tablespoon coconut oil
- 6 bone-in chicken leg quarters

Instructions:

1. Preheat the oven to 400°F.
2. Combine the sweet potatoes, broccoli, zucchini, carrots, and onions in a large bowl.
3. Toss in the chicken broth, rosemary, thyme, salt and pepper.
4. Spread the vegetable mixture in a large glass baking dish and set aside.
5. Melt the coconut oil in a large skillet over medium-high heat.
6. Season the chicken with salt and pepper to taste then add it to the skillet in batches.
7. Cook the chicken for 3 minutes on each side to brown it then place it skin-side-down on top of the veggies.
8. Bake for 30 minutes then flip the chicken and bake for another 30 minutes until the juices run clear.
9. Let the chicken rest for 5 minutes then serve hot with the roasted veggies.

Cilantro Turkey Burgers

Servings: 6

Ingredients:

- 1 ½ pounds lean ground turkey
- 1 cup fresh chopped cilantro
- ½ cup diced red onion
- 2 cloves minced garlic
- ¼ cup gluten-free breadcrumbs
- 1 large egg, whisked
- Salt and pepper to taste

Instructions:

1. Preheat your broiler to low heat and line a broiler pan with foil.
2. Combine the turkey, cilantro, red onion, and garlic in a mixing bowl.
3. Mix in the breadcrumbs, egg and season with salt and pepper, mixing it all by hand.
4. Divide the mixture into 6 even portions, shaping each one into a patty.
5. Place the patties on the broiler pan and cook for 5 to 7 minutes on each side until cooked through.
6. Serve the burgers on toasted gluten-free sandwich buns with your choice of toppings.

Balsamic Glazed Salmon

Servings: 4

Ingredients:

- 4 (6-ounce) boneless salmon fillets
- Salt and pepper
- 1 teaspoon butter

- 2 cloves minced garlic
- ¼ cup balsamic vinegar
- 1 tablespoon white wine
- 1 tablespoon Dijon mustard

Instructions:

1. Preheat the oven to 425°F and line a baking sheet with foil.
2. Season the salmon fillets with salt and pepper then place them on the baking sheet.
3. Melt the butter in a small saucepan over medium heat then add the garlic and cook for 2 minutes until fragrant.
4. Stir in the balsamic vinegar, white wine, Dijon mustard, salt, and pepper.
5. Simmer the mixture until it reduces by half or thickens to coat the back of a spoon.
6. Brush the glaze over the salmon then bake for 12 to 16 minutes until cooked to the desired level.
7. Serve the salmon fillets hot drizzled with extra glaze.

Cheesy Chicken Casserole

Servings: 6 to 8

Ingredients:

- 2 boneless skinless chicken breasts, cut in half
- 1 (14-ounce) can diced tomatoes
- 1 (15-ounce) can black beans, rinsed and drained
- 1 jalapeno, seeded and minced
- 1 (18.5-ounce) can chicken tortilla soup
- 1 teaspoon chili powder
- 1 teaspoon dried oregano
- 8 (6-inch) corn tortillas
- 8 ounces shredded cheddar or Mexican-style cheese

Instructions:

1. Preheat the oven to 375°F and grease a 9x13-inch baking dish with cooking spray.
2. Bring a pot of salted water to boil then add the chicken breast halves.
3. Boil the chicken until it is no longer pink in the middle then drain and let sit until cool enough to handle.
4. Once the chicken is cooled, shred it by hand into a medium-sized bowl.
5. Add the tomatoes, beans, and jalapeno along with 1 cup of the soup.
6. Toss everything together with the chili powder and oregano.
7. Spread the rest of the soup in the baking dish then add a layer of tortillas.
8. Spoon half the chicken mixture over the tortillas and top with one-third of the shredded cheese.
9. Repeat the layers, ending with a layer of cheese, then bake for 20 minutes or until the cheese is slightly browned.
10. Let the casserole cool for 10 to 15 minutes before serving.

BBQ-Glazed Meatloaf

Servings: 6 to 8

Ingredients:

- 1 tablespoon olive oil
- 1 medium yellow onion, diced
- 1 pound lean ground beef
- 1 pound lean ground pork
- ½ cup gluten-free breadcrumbs
- 1 large egg, whisked
- 3 tablespoons skim milk
- 2 tablespoons ketchup

- 1 tablespoon Dijon mustard
- ¾ teaspoon salt
- ¼ teaspoon pepper
- ½ cup BBQ sauce
- 1 tablespoon brown sugar

Instructions:

1. Preheat the oven to 350°F and line a baking sheet with foil.
2. Heat the oil in a skillet over medium-high heat.
3. Add the onions and cook until they are tender, about 6 to 8 minutes.
4. Combine the ground pork and ground beef in a mixing bowl then sprinkle with gluten-free breadcrumbs.
5. Mix the meat and breadcrumbs together by hand then stir in the cooked onions along with the egg, milk, ketchup, mustard, salt, and pepper.
6. Shape the meat mixture into a loaf in the middle of the foil-lined baking sheet.
7. Combine the BBQ sauce, and brown sugar in a bowl then spread it over the meatloaf.
8. Bake the meatloaf uncovered for about 1 hour to 1 hour 15 minutes until the meat is cooked through – it should have an internal temperature of 160°F.
9. Transfer the meatloaf to a cutting board and let it rest for about 5 minutes before slicing it to serve.

Avocado Chocolate Mousse

Servings: 6

Ingredients:

- 6 ounces semisweet chocolate, chopped
- 1 ½ teaspoons vanilla extract

- 3 ripe avocados, pitted and chopped
- ¼ cup unsweetened cocoa powder
- 6 tablespoons skim milk
- 1 tablespoon agave syrup
- Pinch salt

Instructions:

1. Fill a saucepan with 1 to 2 inches of water then place a heat-proof bowl over it.
2. Bring the water in the saucepan to a simmer and place the chopped chocolate in the heat-proof bowl.
3. Let the chocolate melt completely then remove from heat and stir in the vanilla extract.
4. Place the avocado in a food processor then pour in the melted chocolate along with the other ingredients.
5. Blend the mixture until smooth and well combined then spoon into dessert cups.
6. Chill the mousse until ready to serve then top with a dollop of whipped cream.

Chocolate Strawberry Cupcakes
Servings: 12

Ingredients:

- 3 cups almond flour
- ¼ cup cocoa powder, unsweetened
- ½ teaspoon baking soda
- ¼ teaspoon salt
- 3 large eggs, whisked
- ½ cup honey
- ¼ cup melted butter
- 1 teaspoon vanilla extract
- 1 cup fresh diced strawberries

Instructions:

1. Preheat the oven to 325°F and line the cups of a regular muffin pan with paper liners.
2. In a large mixing bowl, whisk together the almond flour, cocoa powder, baking soda, and salt.
3. In a separate bowl, beat together the eggs, melted butter, honey, and vanilla extract.
4. Stir the wet ingredients into the dry ingredients until smooth and well combined.
5. Fold in the diced strawberries then spoon the batter evenly into the prepared pan.
6. Bake for 22 to 25 minutes until a knife inserted in the center of a cupcake comes out clean.
7. Let the cupcakes cool for 5 minutes then remove to a wire rack and cool the rest of the way.
8. Frost the cupcakes as desired when they are fully cooled.

Ginger Peach Crisp

Servings: 6

Ingredients:

- 8 large ripe peaches, pitted and chopped
- 1 cup gluten-free rolled oats
- ½ cup almond flour
- ½ cup chopped pecans
- ¼ cup brown sugar, packed
- ¼ cup coconut oil

Instructions:

1. Preheat the oven to 350°F and grease a casserole dish with cooking spray.
2. Spread the chopped peaches in the casserole dish.

3. Combine the gluten-free oats with the almond flour, pecans, brown sugar, and salt.
4. Mix the coconut oil in by hand until it forms a crumbled mixture.
5. Spread the crumbled mixture over the fruit in an even layer.
6. Bake the crisp for 40 to 45 minutes until the fruit is bubbling and the top of the crisp is browned.
7. Let the crisp cool for a few minutes then spoon into bowls and serve with ice cream.

Coconut Flour Fudge Brownies

Servings: 10 to 14

Ingredients:

- 24 ounces semisweet chocolate, chopped
- 5 large eggs, whisked
- 3/4 cup coconut oil
- ¾ cup agave syrup
- 1 tablespoon vanilla extract
- 1 cup coconut flour
- ½ teaspoon baking soda
- Pinch salt

Instructions:

1. Preheat the oven to 325°F and grease a 9x13-inch baking pan with cooking spray.
2. Fill a saucepan with 1 to 2 inches of water then place a heat-proof bowl over it.
3. Bring the water in the saucepan to a simmer and place the chopped chocolate in the heat-proof bowl.
4. Let the chocolate melt completely then remove from heat and stir in the eggs, coconut oil, agave syrup and vanilla extract.
5. Combine the coconut flour, baking soda, and salt in a mixing bowl.

6. Stir the dry ingredients into the melted chocolate mixture until just combined.
7. Spread the batter in the prepared baking pan and bake for 50 to 60 minutes until a knife inserted in the center comes out clean.
8. Cool the brownies completely before cutting to serve.

Honey Coconut Cupcakes
Servings: 12

Ingredients:

- 3 cups almond flour
- ½ teaspoon baking soda
- ¼ teaspoon salt
- 3 large eggs, whisked
- ½ cup honey
- ¼ cup melted butter
- 2 tablespoons lemon juice
- 1 tablespoon lemon zest
- 1 teaspoon vanilla extract
- ½ cup shredded unsweetened coconut

Instructions:

1. Preheat the oven to 325°F and line the cups of a regular muffin pan with paper liners.
2. In a large mixing bowl, whisk together the almond flour, baking soda, and salt.
3. In a separate bowl, beat together the eggs, melted butter, honey, lemon juice, lemon zest, and vanilla extract.
4. Stir the wet ingredients into the dry ingredients until smooth and well combined.
5. Fold in the shredded coconut then spoon the batter evenly into the prepared pan.

6. Bake for 22 to 25 minutes until a knife inserted in the center of a cupcake comes out clean.
7. Let the cupcakes cool for 5 minutes then remove to a wire rack and cool the rest of the way.
8. Frost the cupcakes as desired when they are fully cooled.

Conclusion

Celiac disease affects more than 3 million Americans, though many of the people who have it remain undiagnosed for years at a time. Many people who have celiac disease either don't present with symptoms or their symptoms develop slowly over time. You might assume that a disease triggered by the consumption of a certain food would present with mostly digestive symptoms, but that is often not the case. Celiac disease symptoms in children are primarily digestive, but adults tend to present with other symptoms such as chronic fatigue, brain fog, joint pain, headaches, and changes in weight or mood.

What many people do not realize is that celiac disease is an autoimmune condition – it is very different from gluten sensitivity or gluten intolerance. For people with celiac disease, following a gluten-free diet is the only effective form of treatment available. It is important to remember, however, that you shouldn't just switch to buying the gluten-free version of your regular foods, assuming that they will be healthy or somehow help you to magically lose weight – this is a common misconception among people who think of the gluten-free diet as a fad diet. What you need to know is that gluten-free versions of processed foods and convenient foods are just as high in sugar and fat as their regular counterparts.

If you suffer from celiac disease, it is up to you to stick to a gluten-free diet. You are responsible for your own health and well-being, so don't take your health for granted! While you might not experience serious side effects from continuing to eat small amounts of gluten, you will be doing damage to your small intestine – damage that could take years to heal. The longer you continue to eat gluten, the more you delay that healing! If you want to start feeling better, your only option is to go completely gluten-free.

Hopefully, by now, you have a more thorough understanding of what celiac disease is and how it affects the body. This is not just another intestinal disorder that will go away on its own – it is a chronic condition that has no cure but which can go into remission with commitment to a gluten-free diet. If you have celiac disease, use the information provided in this book to become your own health advocate. Take steps to protect yourself from gluten exposure and consider whether you should have your children, or other family members tested.

Most of all, try to enjoy the gluten-free diet! Learn how to use gluten-free flour alternatives and other naturally gluten-free ingredients to create healthy, delicious meals and use the recipes provided in this book as a starting point. Enjoy!

References

"10 Gluten-Free Whole Grains You Probably Weren't Aware Of."
Clark. <http://www.clark.com/10-gluten-free-whole-grains-you-
probably-werent-aw>

"Celiac Disease Facts and Figures." The University of Chicago
Medicine. <https://www.cureceliacdisease.org/wp-
content/uploads/341_CDCFactSheets8_FactsFigures.pdf>

"Celiac Disease: Fast Facts." Beyond Celiac.
<https://www.beyondceliac.org/celiac-disease/facts-and-figures/>

"Celiac Disease Treatment and Follow-Up." Celiac Disease
Foundation. <https://celiac.org/celiac-disease/understanding-celiac-
disease-2/treating-celiac-disease/>

"Celiac Disease Symptoms and Conditions Checklist." Celiac
Disease Foundation. <https://celiac.org/celiac-
disease/resources/checklist/>

"Celiac Disease Symptoms Checklist." Beyond Celiac.
<https://www.beyondceliac.org/celiac-disease/symptoms-checklist/>

"Complications of Celiac Disease." Everyday Health.
<http://www.everydayhealth.com/celiac-disease/celiac-disease-
complications.aspx>

"Myths About Celiac Disease." Beyond Celiac.
<https://www.beyondceliac.org/celiac-disease/myths/>

"Other Conditions with Symptoms Similar to Celiac Disease."
WebMD. <http://www.webmd.com/digestive-disorders/celiac-
disease/other-conditions-with-symptoms-similar-to-celiac-disease>

"Recovering from Gluten Contamination." Three Bakers.
<https://threebakers.com/recovering-from-gluten-contamination/>

"Risk Factors for Celiac Disease." *Italian Journal of Pediatrics*. 2015; 41:57.
<https://www.ncbi.nlm.nih.gov/pmc/articles/PMC4535670/>

Roddick, Julie. "Autoimmune Disease." Healthline. <http://www.healthline.com/health/autoimmune-disorders?m=0#Overview1>

"Screening." Celiac Disease Foundation. <https://celiac.org/celiac-disease/understanding-celiac-disease-2/diagnosing-celiac-disease/screening/>

"Sources of Gluten." Celiac Disease Foundation. <https://celiac.org/live-gluten-free/glutenfreediet/sources-of-gluten/>

"Symptoms of Celiac Disease, Wheat Allergy, and Non-Celiac Gluten Sensitivity: Which is it?" Healthline. <http://www.healthline.com/health/allergies/gluten-allergy-symptoms?s_con_rec=true&r=01#Overview1>

"Treatment of Celiac Disease and Gluten-Related Disorders." Celiac Support Association. <https://www.csaceliacs.org/treatment_of_celiac_disease.jsp>

"What is Celiac Disease?" Healthline. <http://www.healthline.com/health/celiac-disease-sprue>

42164850R00036